DINOSAUR MAZES

45 Exciting Mazes Packed with Prehistoric Facts

Art by Marc Pattenden
Words by Matt Yeo

ARCTURUS

ARCTURUS

This edition published in 2022 by Arcturus Publishing Limited
26/27 Bickels Yard, 151–153 Bermondsey Street, London SE1 3HA

Author: Matt Yeo
Illustrator: Marc Pattenden
Designer: Mark Golden
Packaged by Cloud King Creative
Paleontology Consultant: Dougal Dixon
Editors: Violet Peto and Felicity Forster
Design Manager: Jessica Holliland
Managing Editor: Joe Harris

ISBN: 978-1-3988-1539-1
CH010109NT
Supplier 29, Date 0422, PI 00001005

Printed in China

CONTENTS

ANCIENT SUPERCONTINENT

The dinosaurs first appeared around 365 million years ago, in the Triassic period. At that time, most of the land on Earth was part of a large continent called Pangaea.

START

Explore Pangaea and make your way from one side of it to the other!

The fossilized remains of similar dinosaurs and ferns found on continents now far apart show that these landmasses were once joined.

Pangaea was located around the equator of the Earth and was surrounded by a massive superocean known as Panthalassa.

Pangaea eventually broke apart into smaller continents around 175 million years ago. This separating of the landmasses is known as continental drift.

Life thrived in Pangaea, from dinosaurs, the first mammals and insects on the land, to corals, sharks, and ichthyosaurs in the sea.

FINISH

DUSTY DESERTS

The climate in Pangaea was hot and dusty. There were no polar ice caps and much of the land was covered in dry deserts.

Help guide the nimble Guaibasaurus (GWEE-bah-SORE-us) across the desert to the safety of its cave!

START

Some dinosaurs, such as the small 1.8 m (5.9 ft) Guaibasaurus, were herbivores that scavenged for roots and leaves!

The first dinosaurs emerged in the Triassic period, including the fearsome Staurikosaurus (STOR-ik-oh-SORE-us) or "Southern Cross lizard."

Adult Mussaurus
(moo-SORE-us) may have
grown to 3 m (10 ft)
in length, but scientists
named it the "mouse
lizard" as only
small baby skeletons
have been found.

FINISH

Although it had long
canine teeth, Lycorhinus
(LIKE-oh-RYE-nus) was also
a herbivore. Its fossils were
found in what is
now South Africa.

GOING GREEN

While much of Pangaea was covered in deserts, vast areas also saw vegetation grow. Many species of horsetails and lush ferns evolved.

Vegetation thrived in the hot and humid conditions. Seed plants such as cycads, ginkgoes, conifers, and seed ferns were a tasty treat for giant Blikanasaurus (BLIK-ah-nah-SORE-us).

Thecodontosaurus (THEEK-oh-DON-toh-SORE-us) had a fairly short neck, with a large skull, and big eyes. Its tail was longer than its head, neck, and body combined!

Make your way through the thick undergrowth and keep an eye out for any hungry dinosaurs!

START

A huge plant eater,
Massospondylus
(mas-oh-SPON-di-lus)
could grow to between
4-6 m (13-20 ft)
in length!

Heterodontosaurus
(HET-er-oh-DON-toh-SORE-us),
meaning "different toothed lizard"
got its name thanks to the variety
of different-shaped teeth
in its mouth.

FINISH

NORTH AND SOUTH POLES

The Triassic period was much hotter than it is today. In fact, it was so much warmer at the poles that forests would have grown, allowing life to flourish!

Explore the temperate polar regions, where many different species of dinosaur lived and hunted.

START

The large Ruehleia (roo-LEE-ah) was a huge herbivore that fed on shrubs and other small plants. It mostly lived in and around lakes and swamps.

Only one complete fossilized skeleton of a Pisanosaurus (PIE-san-oh-SORE-us) has ever been found. It is believed to have been a small, lightly built herbivore.

Euskelosaurus
(YOO-skel-oh-SORE-us)
had special bowlegs,
which paleontologists
believe helped it
cope with its
huge body.

Agrosaurus (AG-roh-SORE-us)
means "field lizard." From
the few remains that have
been discovered, scientists
think this dinosaur may have
been an omnivore.

FINISH

11

ROCKY LANDSCAPE

Some Triassic environments offered little shelter or food. Brave dinosaurs that lived in these areas had to fight for survival!

Anchisaurus (AN-kee-SORE-us) spent much of its time on four legs, but could also rise to reach food by standing on its muscular hind legs!

Coelophysis (SEE-loh-FISE-iss) was an early meat-eating dinosaur which relied on its speed and agility to catch small insects and reptiles.

Dodge the hungry predators and hide behind rocks to make it all the way to the watering hole!

START

Little is known about Dolichosuchus (DOLL-ich-oh-SUCH-us), as only part of a leg bone has been found by paleontologists. Its name means "long crocodile."

FINISH

Alwalkeria (al-WALL-ke-REE-ah) was a very early type of dinosaur known as a theropod. It was about 50 cm (1.6 ft) long and weighed about as much as a turkey!

RISE OF THE DINOSAURS

Dinosaurs dominated the deserts of Pangaea and thrived in the arid interior. They also began to diversify, resulting in many different types emerging.

Can you make it through this dusty desert maze without getting caught by the massive Aliwalia rex (ah-lee-WAHL-ee-uh REX)?

START

Paleontologists believe that Plateosaurus (PLAT–ee–oh–SORE–us) may have lived in herds for protection from larger dinosaurs.

Lesothosaurus (leh–SO–toh–SORE–us) was small and agile and had five fingers on each hand. It used its small grinding teeth to chew up plant material.

Not much is known about
Aliwalia rex, but it's possible
it may have been a very large
carnivore at up to 6 m
(19.7 ft) in length!

FINISH

Ischisaurus
(ISS-kee-SORE-us) was
a small meat eater that
spent most of its time on
four legs, but could also stand
up on two legs when needed.

TRIASSIC SHORELINE

Life thrived along the coast during this period, with many different creatures living on the shore and near the sea.

Navigate along the shoreline from the cliffs and into the sea. Watch out for all sorts of snapping dinosaurs along the way!

START

The quick-moving Dilophosaurus (die-LOFF-oh-SORE-us) had thin bony crests on its head for displaying to potential mates.

Liliensternus (LIL-ee-en-SHTURN-us) was a small carnivore that had distinctive fin-like crests along its snout. It was an agile and fast hunter.

At over 10 m (33 ft) in length, Camelotia (CAM-ee-LOH-tee-ah) was one of the largest dinosaurs of the Triassic period!

FINISH

A carnivore with lots of sharp teeth, Dilophosaurus had a kink in its upper jaw, which may be a hint that it ate certain kinds of food.

INTO THE MOUNTAINS

Pangaea was built of many earlier continents coming together, with mountains forming along the joins.

A small scavenger, Procompsognathus (pro-COMP-sog-NAY-thus) had long hind legs, short arms, and large clawed hands. It mostly ate insects, lizards, and small prey.

START

Guide the Procompsognathus through the mountain path to reach the rest of its kind.

Velocipes (veh-LOSS-eh-PEES) means "quick foot." It's possible this nimble carnivore could run at fast speeds to catch small animals.

Paleontologists think that Efraasia (eh-FRAH-see-ah) may have used its distinctive thumb claw to defend itself from other dinosaurs.

Melanorosaurus (MEH-lan-or-oh-SORE-us) was a dinosaur known as a sauropod. It could grow to over 12 m (39.4 ft) in length.

FINISH

PREHISTORIC FLOODPLAINS

A vast floodplain ten times the size of the Amazon rain forest existed during the Triassic period. It was roughly a staggering 1.65 million km (1.03 million miles) square!

Follow the path of the river through the floodplain. Try not to get lost along the way!

START

The name Coelophysis (SEE-loh-FISE-us) means "hollow form." This dinosaur's sharp teeth and grasping claws helped it to hold onto its food.

With its whip-like tail and long legs, Chindesaurus (CHIN-deh-SORE-us) was a sleek dinosaur built for speed. It was fast enough to avoid larger dinosaurs too.

A small carnivore, Herrerasaurus (HER-ray-rah-SORE-us) was a nimble hunter with powerful hind legs and three-clawed hands for grabbing.

Eoraptor (EE-oh-RAP-tuhr) had light, hollow bones, and long legs, allowing it to move around quickly while scavenging for scraps of food.

LUSH CONIFER FORESTS

As flowering plants and grass had yet to evolve, much of the planet was covered in vast conifer forests.

The huge Riojasaurus (ree–OH–hah–SORE–us) was over 5.2 m (17 ft) in length. Scientists have found 20 skeletons to date.

Guide the Coloradisaurus (KOH–loh–rah–dih–SORE–us) through the forest to reach the tasty ferns!

START

Small dinosaurs such as Saltopus (SAL–to–PUSS) would scour the forest floors for small insects and other creatures to eat.

Some giant conifer trees could grow as tall as 30 m (98.4 ft). Forests were also covered in now-extinct seed ferns.

FINISH

Eoraptor (EE-oh-RAP-tuhr) was a small sauropodomorph with razor-sharp, backward-curving teeth.

BEAT THE HEAT

Very few species could survive in the heat of the Triassic deserts, but dinosaurs originally evolved to cope with hot desert conditions.

Weave your way through the scorched Triassic desert and make it past all the dinosaurs in one piece!

START

Scientists have discovered that the braincase and neck of Tawa (TAH-wah) was surrounded by air sacs, just like living birds.

Staurikosaurus (STOR-ik-oh-SORE-us) was a small dinosaur known as a theropod. At 2.2 m (7.2 ft) in length, it had sharp teeth and powerful jaws!

Ingentia (in-JEN-she-ah)
means "the first giant,"
and this dinosaur was
huge. It could weigh in at
over 9,000 kg (19,841 lbs)!

Paleontologists think that
Eodromaeus (EE-oh-dro-MAY-us)
may have been able to run at
speeds of up to 32 km
(19.9 miles) per hour, thanks
to its long legs.

FINISH

FIERY VOLCANOES

During the Triassic period, large-scale volcanic activity pushed carbon dioxide into the atmosphere, heating up the planet.

Scientists believe that the heating up of the climate over 201 million years ago caused mass extinctions of many prehistoric species.

Can you make it through this red-hot magma maze? Watch out for rivers of lava and clouds of ash on your way!

START

Climate change caused the sea levels to rise, and up to 100,000 gigatons of carbon dioxide in the air could have made the water more acidic.

Most of Pangaea was hot because the interior of the supercontinent was so far from any cooling effect of the sea.

FINISH

Only the toughest creatures survived this period. Dinosaurs were little affected by the climate changes, and some even flourished!

ON SHAKY GROUND

Toward the end of the Triassic period, shifting tectonic plates and increased seismic activity started to change the landscape of the world.

The Earth's crust is made up of massive rocky plates that are constantly moving and pushing up against each other.

Where these plates meet, pressure can cause them to grind against each other, creating earthquakes and making mountains.

START

Another major earthquake has struck! Guide the dinosaur past the cracks and fissures to safety.

Combined with volcanic eruptions and the heating up of the planet, earthquakes were another major hazard for Triassic life.

Where the land began to separate, the seas began to spread, bringing all sorts of aquatic species with them.

FINISH

MASS EXTINCTION

Many species on the planet were wiped out at the end of the Triassic period. This extinction allowed the dinosaurs to expand and take over.

There are various theories as to why the Triassic extinction event occurred. One possibility is that there may have been a huge asteroid impacting the planet.

Make your way through the devastated extinction landscape as quickly as possible!

START

The Triassic extinction event that occurred about 201 million years ago was a global turning point that resulted in the loss of up to 76% of marine and terrestrial species.

Climate change could also have played a major part in the extinction of life, with rising temperatures, acidic seas, and volcanic eruptions.

FINISH

Some scientists believe the devastation was so severe that it took the Earth over 10 million years to recover from the damage!

SPLITTING CONTINENTS

By the end of the Triassic period, the Earth's landmasses had begun to break apart and Pangaea split into smaller continents.

START

Follow the shifting continental divide and move through the planet's changing landmasses!

Pangaea started to break apart around 200 million years ago, eventually forming the modern continents and Atlantic and Indian oceans.

The outer shell of the Earth, or lithosphere, is made up of large rigid plates. The splitting apart of these is known as plate tectonics.

Scientists believe that the planet's tectonic plates have been joined together and broken apart several times since the Earth's formation.

The process of these tectonic plates being merged and separated is known as a "supercontinent cycle."

FINISH

SURVIVAL OF THE FITTEST

The breakup of Pangaea saw the start of the Jurassic period. Hot and dry climates gave way to a humid subtropical world.

Monolophosaurus (MON–oh–LOW–foh–SORE–us) was a large carnivore with a long bony crest on its head, probably for displaying to potential mates.

Proceratosaurus (PRO–seh–RAT–oh–SORE–us) was one of the many species of dinosaur that managed to flourish in the Jurassic period.

START

Can you survive the journey through this lush prehistoric world packed with all kinds of new dinosaurs?

This was truly the age of the dinosaurs, as massive plant-eating sauropods like Cetiosaurus (SEE-tee-oh-SORE-us) roamed the land!

FINISH

A tough mammal with a large snout and strong backbone, Morganucodon (Mor-gun-YOU-coh-DON) lived in and out of water.

EVOLVE TO SURVIVE

Dinosaurs from the Triassic continued to evolve in the Jurassic period, spawning creatures of all shapes and sizes.

Make your way past the many species of dinosaur and watch out for all the snapping jaws!

START

Ceratosaurus (seh-RAT-oh-SORE-us) means "horned lizard." This dinosaur had sharp horns on its head and a row of small bony spikes along its back.

Carnosauria (CAR-no-SORE-ee-ah) was a group of large carnivores that included Allosaurus (AL-oh-SORE-us).

One of the largest of the dinosaurs to ever exist, Apatosaurus (ah-PAT-oh-SORE-us) could grow up to 23 m (75.5 ft)!

Stokesosaurus (STOAKS-oh-SORE-us) was an early relative of Tyrannosaurus (tie-RAN-oh-SORE-us).

FINISH

LAURASIA AND GONDWANA

As the continents continued to drift apart, two large landmasses began to form. These would keep separating into the continents we know today.

Trace your path through the newly formed world and explore the Earth's emerging continents!

START

Gone were the deserts of the Triassic period, to be replaced with lush forests of conifers and palm tree–like cycads.

Gondwana, the southern half, split into Antarctica, Madagascar, India, Australia, Africa, and South America.

38

Laurasia, the northern half, began to break up into North America and Eurasia in the mid-Jurassic period.

The oceans were full of an amazingly diverse range of sea life, including Plesiosaurus (PLEH-zee-oh-SORE-us), giant marine crocodiles, and rays.

FINISH

JURASSIC RAIN FOREST

The Jurassic period was dominated by massive sauropods and vicious carnivores—some of the largest dinosaurs that ever lived!

Tread carefully through the humid rain forest and avoid being trampled or ending up as a dinosaur's lunch!

START

One of the largest land animals in history at 26 m (85.3 ft), Barosaurus (BAR-oh-SORE-us) was big enough to scare off most predators!

Dicraeosaurus (die-CREE-oh-SORR-us) had a relatively short neck for a sauropod.

A small dinosaur,
Ornitholestes
(or-NITH-oh-LES-teez),
or "bird robber," may have
worked together in packs to
catch larger prey.

Metriacanthosaurus
(MET-ree-ah-KAN-tho-SORE-us)
was a fearsome medium-sized
theropod that often
lived in pairs.

GREEN DESERTS

The sprawling arid Triassic deserts of China were transformed into lush green landscapes during the Jurassic period.

START

Open plains were the perfect hunting ground for predators. Can you make it past the hungry carnivores to safety?

Reigning supreme in the Jurassic period, Sinraptor (sine-RAP-tuhr) had 9 cm (3.5 in) long teeth for catching its prey!

Only very brave dinosaurs would have challenged the spiked Huayangosaurus (hoy-YANG-oh-SORE-us) to a fight.

Yandusaurus
(YAN–doo–SORE–us)
lived together in herds
to protect themselves
from attacks by larger
dinosaurs.

A small herbivore at
only 1.5 m (4.9 ft)
in length, Agilisaurus
(ah–JILL–ee–SORE–
us) was fast enough to
evade most predators.

FINISH

FOREST LIFE

Huge conifer forests filled with trees and ferns covered much of Laurasia and Gondwana—the perfect dinosaur habitat.

Thanks to its very long neck, Brachiosaurus (BRAK–ee–oh–SORE–us) was able to reach tasty leaves at the tops of the tallest trees.

Head through the thick vegetation of the Jurassic period conifer forest to make it safely out the other side!

START

Elaphrosaurus (EL–ah–froh–SORE–us) had an unusually long body, but short hind legs. It was most likely a carnivore or omnivore.

At over 26 m (85.3 ft), Diplodocus (dip-LOH-doh-kus) had a very weak neck supported by ligaments from its hip to its head.

FINISH

Gargoyleosaurus (GAR-goy-LEE-oh-SORE-us), or "gargoyle lizard," had spiky plates on its back and a bony clubbed tail.

EASY PREY

With so many species of dinosaur in the Jurassic period, there was plenty of food for every creature to eat!

Veterupristisaurus (VET–er–uh–PRIST–ee–SORE–us) was the terror of Jurassic Africa.

Help guide the hungry Coelurus (seel-YEW-rus) through the subtropical forest for a giant feast!

START

Elaphrosaurus had very thin and light bones, which may have made it one of the fastest dinosaurs of this period.

Giraffatitan (ji-RAFF-ah-TIE-tan) was a staggering 23 m (75.5 ft) in length, but only had a very small brain!

Smart predators were wise to keep their distance from the lethal spikes along the back of Kentrosaurus (KEN-troh-SORE-us).

FINISH

JURASSIC TITANS

This era was the age of truly gigantic dinosaurs—colossal giants that are some of the largest species in history!

At over 35 m (114.8 ft) in length, Supersaurus (SOO–per–SORE–us) was a gigantic dinosaur that used its size and large tail to ward off predators.

Can you help the young Dacentrurus (DAH-sen-TROO-russ) safely past the towering sauropods to its mother?

START

Dacentrurus was the first stegosaur (STEG-oh-SORE) ever discovered by paleontologists.

Although not the largest sauropod of the Jurassic period, Euhelopus (YOO-hel-oh-PUSS) could still grow up to 10 m (32.8 ft) in length.

Also known as a dwarf sauropod, Europasaurus (YOO-roh-pah-SORE-us) had a distinctive arched head and long neck.

FINISH

UP IN THE SKY

It wasn't just the land that was filled with strange creatures during the Jurassic period. The sky was crowded with winged beasts too!

START

Guide the pterosaur (TEH-roh-sore) through the clouds back to its nest.

Microraptors (MY-kroh-RAP-tuhrs) had long feathers on all four limbs. Scientists think these dinosaurs may have been capable of guided flight.

Fossils of Archaeopteryx (ARK-ee-OPT-er-iks) show the evolutionary link from non-avian theropod dinosaurs to birds.

Also known as "winged lizards," pterosaurs were relatives of the dinosaurs. They had huge wings that stretched from a long fourth finger to their ankles!

FINISH

The German word for Archaeopteryx is "Urvogel," which translates as "original bird" or "first bird."

UNDER THE SEA

The oceans of the Jurassic period were teeming with all sorts of strange lifeforms, from dinosaurs and sharks to rays and ammonites.

Growing up to 3.3 m (10.8 ft) in length, plesiosaurs (PLEH-zee-oh-SORES) would have been a common sight in Jurassic seas.

Ichthyosaurs (IK-thee-oh-SORES) were fast predatory fish that used their sharp teeth to eat squid and fish.

Which is the correct path for the ammonite (AM-oh-nite) to take through the seas to reach the rest of its school?

START

Ammonites moved through the warm seas by squirting jets of water from their shells!

FINISH

Sharks are some of the Earth's most ancient creatures. They were present in Jurassic seas, and many species are still alive today.

ALL SHAPES AND SIZES

Many paleontologists regard the Jurassic period as the height of the time of the dinosaurs, with a multitude of species appearing.

Guide the Compsognathus (komp-SOG-nah-thus) past the dinosaurs to reach its mate.

START

Paleontologists think that Camptosaurus (KAMP-toh-SORE-us) may have walked on two legs, but also went on four legs when grazing.

Stegosaurus (STEG-oh-SORE-us) may have had huge bony plates on its back and spiked tail, but its brain was about the size of a plum!

A titan of the Jurassic period, Brontosaurus (BRONT–oh–SORE–us) was a massive herbivore over 22 m (72 ft) in length.

A small dinosaur, Compsognathus is known as a hunter of small animals like lizards. The best specimen known has a complete lizard in its stomach!

FINISH

OUT IN THE OPEN

Wild plains of ferns made perfect feeding grounds for plant-eating dinosaurs, but they also made it easier for predators to spot them!

Little is known about Haplocanthosaurus (HAP-loh-kan-tho-SORE-us), but this herbivore was over 21.5 m (70.5 ft) in length.

Guide the Guanlong (GWAN-long) through the wild plains and out the other side.

START

Guanlong had a unique air-filled crest on its head, which earned it the name "crowned dragon."

At over 23 m (75.5 ft) long, Camarasaurus (KAM-uh-ruh-SORE-us) used rows of close-set teeth to strip the leaves from trees and shrubs.

FINISH

One of the first dinosaurs ever discovered, Torvosaurus (TOR-voh-SORE-us) was a large hunter with hook-like claws on each finger.

DOMAIN OF THE DINOSAURS

As the dominant species on the planet, dinosaurs could be found in all environments, from subtropical forests to towering mountains.

Work your way through the winding mountain route, making sure to avoid any unwanted scaly attention!

START

Dicraeosaurus is also known as "forked lizard" due to the forked spines in its backbone.

The teeth of the carnivorous Allosaurus (AL–oh–SORE–us) were curved backwards to stop prey from escaping.

FINISH

Apatosaurus had a huge tail that was like a giant bullwhip, and could make a loud cracking sound of over 200 decibels!

Tanycolagreus (TAN—ee—col—AG—ree—us) had a special upper jaw that allowed it to grip its prey, just like modern—day crocodiles.

TROPICAL HEAT

Due to global warming, temperatures rose significantly during the Jurassic period, making it perfect for all sorts of different species of dinosaur to flourish.

Also known as "savage lizard," Torvosaurus was one of the largest carnivores of the Jurassic period.

Othnielia (OTH-ni-EE-lee-ah) were fast herbivores that relied on their speed and large groups to protect them from predators.

Dash through the humid Jurassic rain forest and make it safely to the end in one piece!

START

Mamenchisaurus
(mah–MEN–chee–SORE–us)
had the longest neck of
any animal that has ever
lived, at over 18 m (59 ft)!

FINISH

A stegosaur with
bony plates and horns,
Yingshanosaurus
(YING–shan–oh–SORE–us)
grew up to 5 m
(16.4 ft) in length.

END OF THE JURASSIC

The Jurassic period came to an end around 145 million years ago, when many living species died out. Scientists have debated the causes of this extinction event.

Some scientists believe the Earth was hit by an asteroid or comet during this time, causing widespread destruction.

Hurry, find shelter! Dash through the bleak landscape, avoiding danger, and try to make it safely past the volcano.

START

Other scientists believe rising carbon dioxide levels increased global warming, making life impossible for many animals.

The increase in CO_2 also resulted in the Earth's oceans becoming much more acidic, wiping out marine life such as ammonites.

FINISH

While most dinosaurs became extinct, some small mammals found safety scurrying around the forest floors.

REIGN OF THE DINOSAURS

The Cretaceous period lasted for roughly 79 million years, and saw many new life forms rise to dominance.

Can you find the correct path through this prehistoric maze? Watch out for hungry dinosaurs of all shapes and sizes!

START

A herbivore that could walk on four or two legs, Iguanodons (ig-WAH-noh-dons) had large thumb spikes for protection.

The ultimate carnivore, Tyrannosaurus rex (tie-RAN-oh-SORE-us REX) was a fierce hunter whose bite was three times more powerful than a lion's!

FINISH

Triceratops (tri–SEH–ra–tops) could have used its horns and bony frill to protect itself from carnivore attacks.

While Tyrannosaurus was the greatest hunter of North America, Giganotosaurus (JIG–ah–NOT–oh–SORE–us) held the same position in the South American continent.

KING OF THE SEAS

A wide diversity of marine animals have ruled the oceans at different times. They came in many unique shapes and sizes.

START

Explore the depths of the prehistoric seas and try to steer clear of any chomping jaws!

One of the largest predators to have ever lived, Megalodon (MEH–guh–luh–DON) could grow to over 18 m (59 ft) in length!

Mosasaurus (MOH–sah–SORE–us) was not a dinosaur, but was more closely related to snakes and monitor lizards.

Prehistoric oceans were full of all kinds of cephalopods, including the vampire squid, Vampyronassa (VAM-pie-ir-oh-NASS-ah).

At around 9.9 m (32.4 ft) in length, Machimosaurus rex (MATCH-ee-mo-SORF-us REX) is the largest sea-dwelling crocodile ever found.

FINISH

ON THE HUNT

There were many large carnivores roaming around in the Cretaceous period, making life very dangerous for smaller dinosaurs!

Slowly make your way out of the conifer forest and past the dinosaurs looking for their next meal!

START

Alamosaurus (AL—uh—mo—SORE—us) was a gigantic plant—eating dinosaur that could reach up to 21 m (69 ft) in length!

One of the largest carnivores of the Cretaceous period, Spinosaurus (SPINE—oh—SORE—us) had a sail—like fin on its back to attract mates.

FINISH

Usually moving around in
herds, Parasaurolophus
(PA–ra–sore–OL–off–us) had
a unique bony crest running
along the top of its head.

An unusual dinosaur,
Brachylophosaurus
(BRAK–ee–LOF–oh–
SORE–us) had a bony
crest over its skull,
a beak, and long
forearms.

DINO-SOARS

Flying reptiles were a common sight in the Cretaceous period, but the skies were also filled with the first feathered birds!

Help the Pteranodon (teh-RAH-no-don) swoop, dive, and glide its way to the safety of its nest on the craggy cliffs.

START

Quetzalcoatlus (KWETS-ul-koh-AT-lus) was a massive flying creature that was almost the same size as Hatzegopteryx.

With a wingspan of over 12 m (39.4 ft), Hatzegopteryx (HATS-egg-OPP-ter-iks) is one of the largest known flying animals to have ever existed.

Pteranodons had no teeth, but used their sharp beak to catch fish. Their wingspan was over 5.5 m (18 ft).

Hesperornis (HESS-per-OR-nis) was a large flightless bird with a flattened tail to help it paddle on the surface of the sea.

FINISH

POLAR FORESTS

Although not as hot as in the Triassic and Jurassic periods, the high temperatures in the polar regions prevented ice and snow from forming.

A huge herbivore with a long neck and tail, Antarctosaurus (ant-ARK-toh-SORE-us) may also have had bony plates.

START

Help guide the young Styracosaurus (sty-RAK-oh-SORE-us) through the polar landscape to reach its mother!

Although a dangerous predator with a spiked skull and powerful jaws, Carnotaurus (KAR-noh-TORE-us) only had very tiny wrist-like arms!

Usually staying together in herds for protection, Timimus (tee-MY-mus) was one of the fastest dinosaurs.

Paleontologists suggest that Styracosaurus was probably a very social animal that stayed together with its mates and young.

FINISH

ROCKY CLUES

Scientists have been able to work out much about prehistoric life thanks to minerals, sediment, and deposits left behind in rock formations!

Follow the winding path through the surrounding rocks and work out the route through the stony environment.

START

Aucasaurus (AW–ka–SORE–us) was only around 5 m (16.4 ft) in length, but had powerful jaws for grabbing prey.

Tanius (TAHN–ee–us) was a herbivore and the first dinosaur fossil to be discovered by a Chinese scientist.

FINISH

Paleontologists suspect that Rugops (ROO-gops) may have been a scavenger dinosaur rather than catching its own prey.

Although slightly smaller than a T. rex, Tarbosaurus (TAR-boh-SORE-us) still had a bone-crushing bite and fast legs.

DEEP IN THE FOREST

Many different species of dinosaur often lived together in the same habitat, sharing food and water sources.

START

Follow the path of the river through the subtropical forest to find your way out of this challenging maze!

Stenonychosaurus (steh-NON-ee-coh-SORE-us) was a fast and deadly predator. Scientists suspect that it may actually have been covered in feathers!

It may have been a slow-moving plant eater, but Ankylosaurus (AN-kee-loh-SORE-us) had spiked plates and a club tail for protection.

At over 35 m (114.8 ft) in length, Argentinosaurus (AR-juhn-TEE-no-SORE-us) is the largest land animal ever found!

Among the most ferocious predators of the Cretaceous period, Albertosaurus (al-BURT-oh-SORE-us) had saw-like teeth for tearing apart prey!

FINISH

STAYING ALERT

Dinosaurs often lived near a source of water for survival, but they had to keep an eye out for any lurking predators!

Tread carefully through the Cretaceous marshland maze, watching out for any dinosaurs hidden in the forest.

START

Deinocheirus (DINE–oh–KIRE–us) was a strange-looking dinosaur, with huge clawed hands, a beaked head, and a hump like a camel!

Corythosaurus (Koh–RITH–oh–SORE–us) is also known as "helmet lizard," due to the bony crest on its head.

A scavenger with teeth and
two-fingered front limbs,
Gorgosaurus (GOR-goh-SORE-us)
could reach up to 9 m
(29.5 ft) in length.

FINISH

Hypacrosaurus
(hi-PAK-roh-SORE-us)
had a short toothless
beak, but almost 40
rows of cheek teeth
for munching plants.

RISE OF THE MAMMALS

Dinosaurs weren't the only species to be found during the Cretaceous period. All sorts of mammals lived alongside them and even hunted small dinos.

Troodon (TROH-oh-don) was a small dinosaur with a very large brain for its size. It was only about as smart as a chicken, though!

Liaoconodon (LIE-ah-oh-CON-oh-don) was a semi-aquatic mammal that had a long body and paddle-like limbs.

START

Quickly guide the Liaoconodon through the forest undergrowth and make it safely into the water.

Repenomamus robustus
(REP-un-oh-MAM-us ro-BUST-us)
was a badger-sized mammal
about 1 m (3.3 ft)
in length.

Fossilized skeletons of
Repenomamus robustus
suggest it was a
carnivore that preyed
on smaller animals.

FINISH

A TIME OF CHANGE

Toward the end of the Cretaceous period, even more diverse dinosaur species emerged, including large feathered varieties!

Work out the best route to make it through the dry riverbed. Watch out for dinosaurs along the way!

START

A large feathered and flightless dinosaur, Citipati (CHIT-ee-PAH-tee) was around 2.7 m (9 ft) in length and weighed less than a pig!

Around the size of a chicken, Buitreraptor (BWEE-tree-RAP-tuhr) probably only hunted lizards and small mammals.

As only the skull of Abelisaurus (ah-BELL-ee-SORE-us) has been found, little is known about this carnivore, but it did have a head crest and small teeth.

FINISH

Also known as "small-horned face," Bagaceratops (BAG-ah-SEH-rah-tops) emerged late in the Cretaceous period.

SWAMP THINGS

Warm, moist environments allowed the first flowering plants to appear, and bees and snakes began to evolve.

The large bony crest on the head of Lambeosaurus (lam-BEE-oh-SORE-us) may have been used to make sounds or enhance the dinosaur's sense of smell.

The flat, wedge-shaped skull of Homalocephale (HOME-ah-loh-SEFF-ah-LEE) may have protected its skull when headbutting.

START

Help guide the buzzing bee through the muddy swamp to reach the tasty nectar in the flowers!

Hadrosaurus (HAD-roh-SORE-us) was a duck-billed dinosaur that could grow to 7.6 m (25 ft) in length. Its name means "bulky lizard."

One of the largest spiked dinosaurs, Ankylosaurus (AN-kee-loh-SORE-us) had a huge bone club tail for protection.

FINISH

TREES OF TOMORROW

In the dense and humid subtropical forests of the Cretaceous period, close relatives of living redwoods, pine and yew grew.

Explore the many different species of trees in the Cretaceous forest as you make your way through the maze.

START

Paleontologists have discovered that Saltasaurus (SAL–tah–SORE–us) may have had bony plates for protection.

Edmontonia (ED–mon–TONE–ee–ah) was a heavily spiked herbivore that would stand and fight instead of running away!

At around 30.5 m (100 ft) on length, Ultrasaurus (UL-tra-SORE-us) was one of the largest sauropods of the Cretaceous period.

Although probably a herbivore, Therizinosaurus (THER-uh-ZEEN-oh-SORE-us) had the longest claws of any known animal. They were 60 cm (2 ft) in length!

FINISH

CONTINENTAL DIVIDE

The Cretaceous period ended around 66 million years ago. By this point, the continents had drifted even farther apart.

Rising sea levels during this time meant that landmasses began to shrink further, as some areas were flooded by the oceans.

START

Explore the constantly shifting continents of the planet as the prehistoric world continues to grow and change!

Australia was still joined to Antarctica at this time, and they were both barely attached to what are now North and South America.

FINISH

Madagascar broke away from Africa during the late Cretaceous period, and Greenland separated from North America.

Although the end of the Cretaceous period was the coolest, the planet was still much warmer than it is today.

TWILIGHT OF THE DINOSAURS

After millions of years ruling the Earth, the time of the dinosaurs was almost at an end. With it would come a period of huge global change.

The most powerful land predator Tyrannosaurus rex, "king of the tyrant lizards," ruled the Cretaceous period.

Run with the speedy Dakotasaurus (duh-KOH-tuh-SORE-us) through the sunset landscape and reach its mate near the volcano.

START

The spear-like skull of the Pteranodon meant it was adapted for diving from a great height to catch fish.

FINISH

Some scientists believe that Dakotasaurus was nocturnal, with larger eyes for hunting in the dark!

As well as offering protection, the bony plates of Ankylosaurus helped camouflage it from predators.

END OF THE WORLD

When the Cretaceous period came to an end, up to 80% of all animals and many plant species were wiped out.

Avoid becoming extinct by racing through this tricky maze and staying clear of the huge asteroid!

START

Known as the K-T extinction, this event changed the future of the planet for many millions of years to follow.

Some scientists think this extinction event could have been caused by diseases, global warming, or earthquakes.

One popular theory is
that the Earth was hit
by a massive asteroid
which threw dust into
the atmosphere and
blocked out the Sun.

The only surviving
descendants of
dinosaurs and their
kin are the birds
and crocodiles!

ANSWERS

4–5

6–7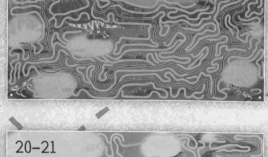

8–9

10–11

12–13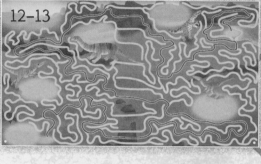

14–15

16–17

18–19

20–21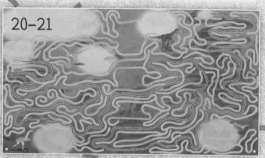

22–23

24–25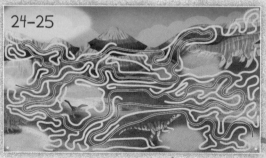

26–27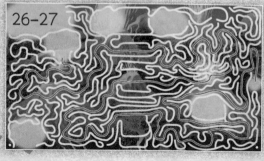

28–29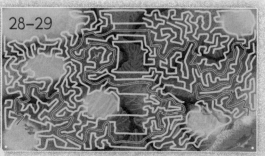

30–31

32–33

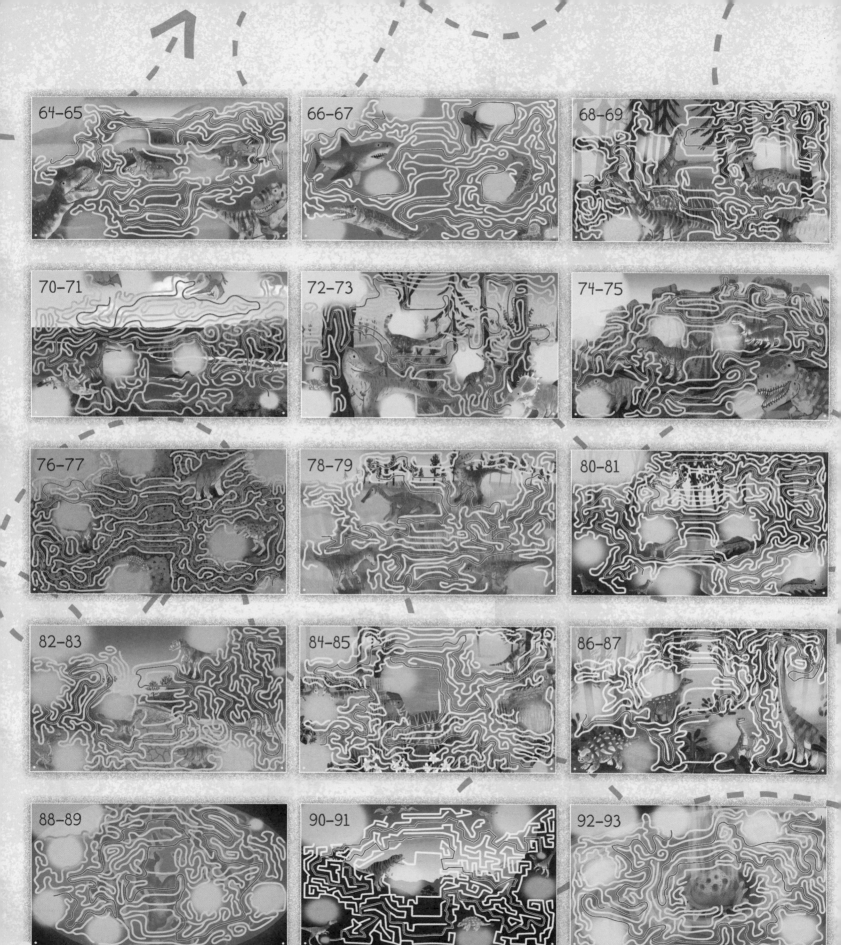